# On Wonder

© Vanessa Proctor   2024

All rights reserved. Except for appropriate use in a book review, no part of this publication may be reproduced, stored in a retrieval system, or transmitted in any form or by any means, without the prior permission of the publisher, or in the case of photocopying or reprographic copying, a licence from the Copyright Agency of Australia.

**On Wonder**

ISBN 9781763653078

Cover Art   Vanessa Proctor

Cover Design   Alex Baird

Walleah Press
South Launceston
Tasmania, Australia 7249

www.walleahpress.com.au
ralph.wessman@walleahpress.com.au

**Walleah Press**

# On Wonder

*Vanessa Proctor*

# Contents

| | |
|---|---|
| In the Park | 1 |
| Harmony | 2 |
| Emergence | 3 |
| Fracture | 5 |
| Story Café | 7 |
| At the Australian Museum | 8 |
| Natural History Museum | 9 |
| Beading | 10 |
| Wegberg 1980 | 11 |
| Waking Dream | 12 |
| Ashridge Forest | 13 |
| On Wonder | 14 |
| A dragonfly | 15 |
| Expansions | 16 |
| Hemispheres | 17 |
| Helleborus Niger | 19 |
| Mandragora | 20 |
| Cutting Down the Tulip Tree | 21 |
| The Garden Pond | 22 |
| Citizen Science | 23 |
| Through My Window | 24 |
| A Passing Moment | 25 |
| Overflow | 26 |
| Bathroom Orchid | 27 |
| Transplanted | 28 |
| Cicada Shells | 29 |
| Wildflower Bees | 30 |
| Chinese Garden of Friendship | 31 |

| | |
|---|---|
| All in the Timing | 32 |
| Sisyphus | 33 |
| Crossing the Harbour Bridge | 34 |
| Double Bay | 35 |
| Sussex Inlet | 36 |
| Whale Psalm | 37 |
| Fitzroy Falls | 39 |
| Sunday Afternoon at Lake Burley Griffin | 40 |
| A Walk in the Fog and Snow, Kinglake | 41 |
| Fingal Spit | 42 |
| On Flying to Launceston for the Tasmanian Poetry Festival | 43 |
| Design Tasmania | 44 |
| Bellinger River | 45 |
| Westward | 46 |
| Cape Naturaliste | 47 |
| Flotsam | 48 |
| Murasaki Shikibu in Service at the Imperial Palace, 1010 | 49 |
| The Scattering of Blossom | 50 |
| A Brief History of Umami | 53 |
| La Cocotte Ronde | 55 |
| Walking Shadow | 56 |
| Florence Fisher, 1872 | 57 |
| The Skating Minister | 58 |
| Darwin's Gardener, 1881 | 59 |
| Parakeets over a London Graveyard | 60 |
| After midnight the streets belong to the foxes | 61 |
| Endangered | 62 |
| Four Minutes | 63 |
| The Sphinx Memorial, Bobbin Head | 64 |
| Endless Night | 66 |
| Hyde Park, Sydney, 1949 | 67 |

| | |
|---|---|
| O Quam Mirabilis Est | 69 |
| Le Stryge | 70 |
| Basement Blues | 72 |
| Old Violin | 73 |
| Caught | 75 |
| Aftermath | 76 |
| Night Vision | 77 |
| Myopia | 78 |
| Orbit | 79 |
| Scenic | 80 |
| In Praise of Ocean Swimmers | 81 |
| The Gift | 82 |
| A Brief Catalogue of Joy | 83 |
| | |
| Publication Credits | 84 |

## ABOUT THE AUTHOR

Vanessa Proctor is an award-winning Australian poet. She has an MA in Creative Writing and her work has been widely published both in Australia and overseas for the last thirty years. She is a foundation member of the Australian Haiku Society and served as its president from 2016 – 2020. Her poetry has been translated into several languages, including Croatian, French, Hungarian, Japanese and Romanian. Her work has also been set to music and is represented on public art installations in New Zealand and Australia. Her previous haiku publications are the chapbook *Temples of Angkor* Sunline Press (2003), the eChapbook *Jacaranda Baby* Snapshot Press (2012) and *Blowing up Balloons: baby poems for parents* Red Moon Press (2017) cowritten with Gregory Piko. This is her first collection of free verse.

*for my parents Edna and George*

## In the Park

trees uncover their skeletons
leaf by leaf, the peeling bark
of the blue gums, the ground
cross-hatched with fallen branches.

The earth is humming
with the energy of the unseen:
wombats in their burrows,
rabbits multiplying,
possums and gliders
in the treetops, spiders
and ants and worms.

Under this cloudless winter sky
everything is stripped down
to reveal this moment,
this place, this now.

## Harmony

They breathe in time,
reminiscent of the litter,
the gentle rhythms of the womb.
Warm fur against warm skin,
a meditation. Lives lived at home
or following the slow burning
campfires of time. Guided
by Sirius they journey, their song
a silent melody of dreaming.
Always the same girl,
her same golden companion.
Dog with girl, girl with dog.

## Emergence

*Everything has been figured out, except how to live.*
                                                  *Jean-Paul Sartre*

You sleep under a blue lamp
in a plexiglass crib,
four days old,
skin yellow with jaundice,
twig-thin arms and legs.

It wasn't meant to start this way –
the confines of the womb
to the special care nursery,
yet you seem unperturbed,
your body folded tightly
into indigo dreams.

Soon I'll take you home,
hold you, get to know you,
from the outside in.

You'll learn the contours of faces,
faces like yours.
There will be words and music.

I'll take you outside.
We'll feel the breadth of the sky,
watch birds, the way
sunlight catches leaves.

There will be new smells,
jasmine from the garden, wet dog,
woodsmoke from winter fires.
We will take it all in.

There will be plenty of milk,
then good solid food.

Sleep, recover,
enjoy the warmth
of the lamp, this time in limbo.
We can wait
and then together
we will make a start on living.

## Fracture

The skin
around her small ankle
is patterned blue,
tight,
swollen.

The x-ray reduces
tissue, bone
to an icy landscape
of light and shadow,
a map for practised eyes.

The fracture is clear
even for the uninitiated,
a horizontal line,
a vertical break,
crevasse,
fissure,
glacial, mysterious,
the purity of bone
amid darkness.

She is comfortable now,
the ankle firmly held
by a cast,
more awkward than
painful.
I determine to become
wheelchair pusher,
crutch instructor,
fetcher, carrier.

There will always be
displacements,
breaks,
widening rifts
pushing us away
from each other.

Alike,
we are both
impatient, impulsive,
stubborn.
There is bound to be
jarring and pain.

I must be patient,
allow her to grow,
steer her away from
the snow and ice
and attempt
to hold it all
together.

## Story Café

*We tell ourselves stories in order to live.*

*Joan Didion*

At a burnished copper table
amid the clink of coffee cups
two women lean in towards
each other. The white-haired one
talks and her companion listens,
*I cry every day, you know.*
*He cries too. What can I do?*

Two milk bottles of dried flowers
away, a mother loudly tells
a colleague about her daughter,
the public speaker, taking exams,
the pressure she feels, the pressure
they all feel. Someone shouts an order
and the coffee machine hisses with steam.

We are sandwiched
between sentences that appear
like glass noodles, transparent,
shiny, temptingly delicious,
bitten off halfway through.

The waitress, with sad eyes
and a shining face, sets down
two steaming bowls of pho.
I look at my son, freshly out
of hospital, his half smile,
his left wrist bandaged tightly
wearing his story.

## At the Australian Museum

You stand proud
in your safari jacket
and dinosaur tail,
then stomp around the hall
with a herd of three-year-olds
roaring ferociously.

On the train to the city
I asked you if dinosaurs
were large or small

and you replied,
after some deliberation,
"very small".
And here you are
squealing with delight at
Jobaria towering above you
and Afrovenator
gnashing its teeth at your side.

It's the dawning of a new age
of tooth and claw, scale and bone
where *muttaburrasaurus* has become
your latest codeword for fun.

## Natural History Museum

We take a trip to the city
on one of those grey autumnal days
where leaves scuttle across
dusty pavements and
pigeons huddle on ledges.

Yet I am all sunshine,
surprised at his attention,
swinging my feet as he ponders
*The Times* crossword.
I watch the fields slip away into brick
and stone, and we emerge blinking,
moles into daylight.
Trotting to keep up with his long legs,
I reach the entrance breathless.

In the cavernous hall,
we stare at ancient bone
wired to ancient bone,
reconstructions of children's nightmares,
tooth and talon, spine and skull,
winged terror suspended
from the domed roof.

T-Rex towers above us,
one eye socket trained on me,
jaws open wide, threatening
to impale me, drag me screaming
back to the stench of the Jurassic.
My father stands by my side,
quiet as usual, his hand
slowly reaching for mine.

## Beading

Beads scatter across the floorboards,
spilling from their packet,
little berries of glass and plastic
roll into random mosaics
on this damp winter's day.
My daughter chooses one,
and then another, making a pile,
threading colour onto lopsided
necklaces and bulky bracelets.

And I think back to the heat
of a Languedoc summer.
My sisters buying melons
from a roadside stall,
heavy and fragrant,
slicing them with
a large-handled knife,
scooping out the seeds,
washing them in river water.

They dried quickly
as we sank our teeth
into the melons' orange flesh.
We pierced the seeds with needles,
strung them together with thread
forming chain after chain
to hang around our nut-brown necks
in a that carefree summer spilling over
with sunshine and salt spray.

## Wegberg 1980

Together we glide
under a brilliant winter sky,
my mother and I,
carving our way
around the frozen lake,
steel blades sharp
as we attempt
figure eights
and arabesques.

But the lake is uneven,
waiting to trip us,
patches of ice darken
among the reeds,
everywhere the warning
end of winter cracks and pops.
We skate on regardless,
quicken our stride,
feel the wind about our ears.

## Waking Dream
*Hope is a waking Dream.*
*Aristotle*

At eleven years old her parents leave
her lost in the company of strangers
with trunk and uniform, in disbelief
she's unprepared for the new arrangement.
The old housemistress, stern and less than fair,
announces, *She does not mix with her peers.*
The boarding house becomes home to nightmares
involving her sentence of seven years.
Somehow she knows in time the hurt will fade
by trying hard to make a few new friends.
She'll study hard and advance in each grade
working towards her exams at the end.
Half term will come with permission to breathe
and dream that one day she'll grow up and leave.

## Ashridge Forest

Sometimes mist would swirl,
soften the darkness
as my father drove me
back to boarding school,
my trunk heavy in the boot,
headlights on high beam.
We hardly spoke, instead
we'd look for fallow deer
eyes shining, ears alert,
seeking out the freshest grass
in moonlit forest clearings.

Once we slowed,
stopped behind a car
to see a doe sprawled
on the tarmac, her eyes
a well of fear, her spindly legs
flailing wildly. Impossible
not to look as the ranger
aimed his rifle, fired,
the shot ringing through
that twilight wood,
cold and hard, the darkness
I had tried to so hard to contain
slowly seeping into everything.

## On Wonder

On reading
Rosemary Dobson's 'Wonder',
my student really doesn't seem to get it,
the idea of wonder,
awe in its original sense.
*Have you never been struck*
*by the beauty of something?* I ask.
*The stars in the night sky?*
*Mountains, the ocean, great art?*
She shrugs.
She's probably messing with me.
I wonder.

## A dragonfly

rests motionless on my finger
as I gently unravel
the spider's silk
that is caught
around its wings and thorax.
   It seems weightless,
with its dark, slender body,
and six fragile legs on my skin.
   I unwrap each strand
until the dragonfly is free,
yet it doesn't move.
We become a stillness
that dissolves into the morning
until  suddenly  it shimmers away
  on brilliant wings
transparent into the blue.

## Expansions

All day I walk
around the house in circles,
leaving jobs half-completed,
thoughts unfinished.
There's no end
to the things
that need
to be done.
The cat sleeps
on the floorboards,
his long ginger fur
rising and falling –
nothing is of consequence
to him.

Outside lorikeets dangle
from camellias, fish skim
the bottom of the pond,
plants grow tangled,
abundant.

Opening the kitchen door,
I can finally breathe,
pulled by the earth
as it tilts
towards the sun.

## Hemispheres

Things are going haywire in my garden.
The winter limes are hanging heavy
on their branches, ripening yellow and green
and beneath, the narcissi have sprouted leaves.

I planted the bulbs years ago,
knowing full well they would never take
in this climate so far from home.
They bloomed in their first spring,
then turned leafy. I should have dug
them up but lacked the heart
and left them to their own confusion.

Now there is one stem, heavy
with seven small white flowers,
obstinately leaning into an autumn landscape
of reddening maples and liquidambars
and the velvet purple of tibouchinas,
reaching for a diminishing sun.

I can't help but think
of April as spring,
no matter how long
I live below the equator.
It's like trying to count
quickly in another language.
No matter how fluent you are,
the numbers never quite stick.

April makes me think of showers
and the promise of warmer days,
but the evenings are drawing in
as we wave goodbye to summer,
and one small stem calls out,

*Where I come from it's spring, remember that.*

Some things are at odds with themselves
in this adopted home. They always will be:
Christmas in the heat of summer
and the tap water spiralling down
the plughole the wrong way.

### Helleborus Niger
*From the Greek 'fatal food, black'*

A swathe of hellebores
leads to my door,
white flowers downcast
in the winter air.
Yet beneath those glossy leaves
the Christmas Rose
is a contradictory plant
that thrives in shade.
Gardeners must take care –
offer prayers to Apollo
(or a favourite saint)
when digging up the hellebore.
If an eagle sees you trowel in hand
you risk a sudden end.
Purgative or poison
the roots may be used in witchcraft
to summon demons or to fight them.
Such a practical plant to grow
in the quiet of the suburbs.

## Mandragora

*So early waking, what with loathsome smells,*
*And shrieks like mandrakes torn out of the earth,*
*That living mortals, hearing them, run mad.*
                    'Romeo and Juliet' William Shakespeare

The mandrake,
a perfect antidote
to noisy neighbours.
Its pale blue flowers
create pleasing borders
along boundary lines,
but beware its powerful magic.
You must dig around the plant
with iron (never with bronze),
plug your ears and those
of your loved ones,
tie your dog's collar to the roots
so your trusted friend
will pull up the plant
when you call him to you.
Remember to squeeze
the mandrake's sap
or it will run away
when you put it down,
shrieking all the way
across the North Shore.

## Cutting Down the Tulip Tree
*Liriodendron tulipifera*

It had been there for decades,
thirty metres tall,
defining our garden,
a favourite of the rosellas
with its attractive autumnal foliage,
the three lobed leaves
turning from green to gold.

But the termites had spent years
feasting on its wood,
leaving a hollow trunk
and dying branches.

Felled swiftly by a chainsaw,
it lay prone on the lawn
and at its tip
we found for the first time
lime green and orange flowers
striking in their last flowering.

## The Garden Pond

tries to recreate a tranquil bush setting
on a small, suburban scale.
River stones are carefully selected,
placed carefully over
the concrete watercourse,
slabs of sandstone arranged just so.
A trickle of stream flows
into an upper pond, wombat-sized,
cascades over chiselled bush rock.
It looks convincing,
but water seeks escape routes everywhere,
veers off through fountain grass,
side-slides the waterfall, is soaked up by stones.
Two pond pumps have already imploded.
Yet in these half-filled pools
magpies come to drink,
skinks shelter under rocks
and in a frothy mess around papyrus
lies the promise of frogs.

## Citizen Science

The first time I tried to record frogsong
it wasn't a frog at all, just an insistent
cricket broadcasting his urgent message
to all the females in the neighbourhood –
stridulating. I know this now for
I am a student of small things, insects,
frogs, a student of one particular frog.
There's much to learn from his persistence.
It's a lonely business being single.

Through the double glazing I hear
him each night, the deer-scarer knock,
the deep tones of the striped marsh frog
welling up from the murk of the backyard
pond. Amphibian, counter-shaded,
he coyly takes cover beneath foliage.
Ours is a starlit after-dinner date
him serenading the world in all his mucousy
glory and I quite clearly the wrong mate.

**Through My Window**

A sandstone wall with terracotta pots
full of succulents overtaken by weeds,
the roots of the enormous palm tree
lifting the capstone. Sunlight playing
on the tendrils of passionfruit vines
colonising the fence and
the tail of a marmalade cat
twitching through the shrubbery.
And there, almost indiscernible,
their heads bobbing as they
follow each other down the side path
in feathery rebellion, a flock
of scratchy-clawed chooks.

## A Passing Moment
*For Jeanette*

She sits at her desk,
my old friend,
and looks out at the garden.
Perhaps she thinks
about pruning the hydrangeas,
notices the triangle of sunlight
edging over the sill.
She opens her notebook
and begins to write.

**Overflow**

Today, everything seems to be spilling over,
the acanthus that grew from wind-blown seed,
its glossy roman leaves reaching over the
terraced wall, the chooks patrolling the fence line,
searching for a way out, the pond fish surfacing
in a pond brimming with last night's rain,
existing in one world, but needing another,
and then there's me, standing in unkempt grass
in a rippling breeze, my basket heavy
with the week's damp clothes, as I peg
sock     after sock     after sock.

## Bathroom Orchid

The phalaenopsis
was an impulse buy,
a small luxury.
A guilty pleasure
placed by the sink
where only I can see,
it counterbalances
reflections of disappointment.
Artifice does not feature
in its language,
it has no critical eye.
Veins of amaranth course
through its petals
which curl towards me,
reaching out its stem
of delicate hearts
and slowly opening buds.
With its glossy leaves
and velvet tongue
it knows exactly
how to be.

**Transplanted**

We gather on the land
of the Darramuragal people
to plant shrubs and trees.

Neighbours, we've all come from
somewhere else, the man who talks
to magpies in Arabic, the woman
who wears dazzling saris,
the opera singer who lives
at number four.

In our hands we hold native plants,
red flowering gum, ironbark
and turpentine, spindly-stemmed,
root balls curled in anticipation.

Someone is boiling the billy
and making damper as we dig
the sandy earth down by the creek.
We plant banksia and wattle with
eucalypts soon to grow skyward,
turning towards the sun like thoughts
of flight, roots reaching out, connecting.

We pause to sip lemon myrtle tea.
In years to come we will say
we planted this tree or that shrub.
How tall they have become,
how shady the canopy.
Above us rosellas flock past,
swoop low in a rush of colour.

## Cicada shells

litter the path
small amber treasures,
brittle and unyielding.
Empty carapaces cling to bark,
        row upon row,
          prehistoric
in their stubbornness,
       the space
where bodies once pulsed
     is filled with air,

wings, fine-veined,
shot through with sunlight.

Then the song
      to end all subterranean dreams
            begins.

It vibrates with the lightness of air,
the motion of flight,
pulses through the undergrowth,

thick with the promise
of long afternoons
and lingering summers
which inevitably end
far too soon.

## Wildflower Bees

The beekeeper unveils his bees
among amber honey jars.
Behind glass
they are imprisoned
in a slice of frustration.
The queen wears
the white spot of privilege,
ceaselessly laying eggs
in each appointed chamber
while the workers agitate in circles,
their pollen baskets empty.

Fair-goers crowd around
for a closer look
at the tangle of black and yellow
heads, legs and wings,
before dispersing to wander
the paths of the garden.

At the end of the day
the beekeeper will return
home with the bees.
In the morning
drones with arcing wings
will rise up to work
every hour of daylight
from banksia to boronia,
myrtle to wattle,
until one by one,
they drop
soundlessly
from the air.

## Chinese Garden of Friendship

It is hard to find peace
in this part of the city
with its endless traffic
and clamour of construction.
Yet, stay long enough
and you'll start to hear
the flow of the cascades.
Pause and you'll notice ibis,
wings outstretched,
balancing on willow tops,
limestone rocks transforming
into dragons
and from the depths
of the Lake of Brightness,
unhurried carp
the colour of sunset
will slowly glide up to you
their mouths wide open.

**All in the Timing**

The same congested intersection
waits for me every morning.
It looks like a roundabout,
but isn't. With traffic
coming from every direction,
no one is quite sure of the rules.
All the time the tension
of impending collision
vibrates through the tarmac.

Decades ago a lover
had a job planting daffodils
in a series of highway roundabouts.
I think of him crouching down, hands
gently planting the bulbs, the traffic
carouselling around him. But he probably
just tossed them in any which way,
covered them over,
thousands more to plant,
leaving them to push their way
up to the light at the centre
of an urban universe, springing
into great wheels of colour
somewhere between stop and go.

## Sisyphus

Frequenting the road to the station,
an elderly man shuffles
painfully up and down the hill
that leads to the highway.

Slowly, stiffly, he pushes out
one leg, then the other,
toes facing outwards
in a slow motion
Chaplinesque walk,
his face a mask
of determination.

Sometimes I pass him again
hours later still shuffling
that endless loop, staggering
up and down that hill,
passed by everyone
in their comfortable cars.

Perhaps he is some kind of metaphor
for all of us trudging through our lives,
doggedly carrying on, facing the elements,
despite the pain, every single day,
to keep the blood flowing,
the heart beating
and the breath coming in.

## Crossing the Harbour Bridge

It's late and there have been some
shared intimacies this evening,
but now there is silence between us
as we drive along the road
that leads us home.

We approach the bridge,
allow it to hold us suspended
over the midnight water of the city
and it's easy not to feel
the weight of it all,
beams, hangers, pylons.
It's easy to ignore
the cantilevered arches
rising above us in cold steel,
two halves brought together
with rivets once white hot.

The bridge's purpose is clear.
It makes its own patterns,
oblique, repetitive, strangely beautiful,
the black sky peering from its ribs.

Above the arc
beams of light illuminate
a flock of silver gulls.
Ghostlike they swoop, freewheel,
snatch moths out of the night.

## Double Bay
*For Nora*

With a bellyful of pierogi
I walk along the foreshore
after visiting a friend.
Half a century divides us,
yet we are united in poetry,
ikebana, ties to the East,
linked by the sinuous thread
of women's lives,
a double helix twisting
in and out of itself,
spirals of sadness replicating
endlessly as the world
keeps on turning.

Seagulls line up
on the storm water pipe,
their backs to the wind
and a pied cormorant,
its white feathers ruffled,
pauses at the end.
It is too murky
for reflections today.
The shag has no choice
but to plunge in, swim
through the dark water,
her wake fanning out
far behind her.

## Sussex Inlet
*For Anna*

We dig our toes into the sand
my friend and I,
the five years we have spent apart
dissipate into the sunlight.

We talk books and writing and
of how things have changed
as my children splash in rockpools
searching for treasure. She finds
fossilised molluscs, sea fans
and ancient trees embedded
into silty rock, picks kelp pods
to taste, salty and sharp
and my son fills his bucket
with muttonbird bones.

The sky brims with semaphore clouds
and the swell rises far out to sea.

## Whale Psalm

We watch humpbacks
through binoculars
on this holiday coast
as they blow, breach,
spy hop far out to sea.
We've been to the museum,
learnt of killer whales,
boats and harpoons,
corsets and lamp oil,
the young colony sustained
by baleen and whale blubber.

We clamber onto a rock shelf,
my daughter and I,
waves washing at our feet
when we see it,
a dorsal fin
and an inky-slick back
not a hundred metres away.
A smaller shape surfaces,
glides alongside –
mother and calf.

Rolling leisurely on her back,
the mother bares the underside
of her pectoral fins,
white against the setting sun,
then shows us her flukes,
perfectly symmetrical
as she dives,
always half-seen,
mysterious.

It is the not-knowing
that strikes me,
the impossibility of getting any closer,
seeing their full shape.
We are willingly ignorant
of the whale's perspective
in a strange and unknown element.
There is no need to dissect
or map out patterns of migration.
We just observe
what they allow us to see.

The whale rumbles gently, deeply,
her calf slapping up against her side,
the closeness of two leviathan bodies.
It is then that I feel it
through the pulse of my daughter's hand,
undeniable,
that swell of undulating joy.

## Fitzroy Falls

over the escarpment,
inevitable, like joy or grief,
rivulets of white spray
cooling the January air.
Gravity grips us with
strange ideas,
pulls us all down,
one way or another,
a rock, a tree, a man.
Only a surprise
of black cockatoos
can suspend its grip
on this landscape
of sandstone, water,
forest and air.
But nothing can tumble
out of place today
when the sky is so blue
with its scudding
rock face clouds
and its watchful gods.

## Sunday Afternoon at Lake Burley Griffin

We've stepped into
Monet's *The Basin at Argenteuil*.
The clouds are the same, great banks
massed low in the summer sky,
small figures boating on the lake,
dinghy sails luffing in the breeze.
Picnickers lounge on grassy banks
and Sunday strollers amble in the shade,
each tree lowering its shadow across the path.

But this is Canberra –
there are no parasols or white Sunday dresses,
most wear baseball caps and running shoes.
Two Buddhist monks smile radiantly
as they pedal their tandem along the path,
orange robes flapping. A family of four,
 conversing in Norwegian, strides
around the lake walking sticks in hand,
a street organ pipes its music into the sunshine.

## A Walk in the Fog and Snow, Kinglake
*After a photograph by Lloyd Godman*

A scattering of snow attempts
to white out memory. Even the fog
is half-hearted this morning.
Charred tree trunks and branches
create sculptures of loneliness and
silence falls heavy on the land.
Yet, shoots, brilliantly new,
are beginning to reach through
the mud. Soon grass will colonise
this place, leaves will create
broad canopies, the green far better
at forgetting than any fog or snow.

## Fingal Spit

The shifting land bridge
links Shark Island to the mainland
in a landscape of soft white sand
and summer-blue skies.

Above volcanic outcrops
of rhyodacite rise, remind us
of the power of fire and ice.

It's low tide,
but not low enough.
There are hidden channels
and swells from both sides
rolling over the thin line of sand.
Everything is governed
by the forces of change,
the synergy of wind and wave
constantly shaping and reshaping.

And so it is with us,
nothing ever still or fixed.
We must be careful
with our timing,
pay attention to the signs,
warnings of drowning,
the risk of being swept away.

Today we admit defeat,
paddle barefoot,
admire the view.
We must wait
for the right time to cross.

## On Flying to Launceston for the Tasmanian Poetry Festival
*For Colin*

Up here, all is light,
rushing air, sunshine glinting
off wingtips. The weight
of every day discarded
in a flash of wheels and wings
as we submit to the forces
of lift and thrust.

Speeding across the Tasman
the coastline froths below us,
the vast glimmering sea
with its intricate coves and bays
and us secured in tight rows
among the cloud drift.

So close now to the awaiting city
and the promise of poets and poetry,
words readying to launch
themselves into full flight.

## Design Tasmania

in the high cool space
of a converted church
rest objects of reverence
cabinets and chests
stools and chairs
lovingly turned
from sassafras
casuarina and myrtle
willing us to reach out
and touch them
in our devotion
the bird's-eye grain
of the Huon pine
ripples over
a cabinet door
polished smooth
glistening
in its pool
of reflection
undulating with
the sanctity and
skill of
the craftsman
this place
a meditation
communing with
the spirits of the forest

## Bellinger River

low tide
a sacred kingfisher darts
from the mangroves

the splash
of a fisherman's lure

sun ripples
tiddlers transparent
above their shadows

from bank to bank
the butcherbird's four note song

voices
across the river
private lives drift my way

shifting colours
pattern the water

lazy afternoon
the slow flap
of a jabiru's wings

the flicker of light
through jetty slats

a gull follows
the river's path
to the sea

## Westward

Driving westward past the tumble of rocks
and sheep of the Yass Valley, fence lines
all but disappear, rough paddocks fan out

into undulating fields of bright rape seed
rivalling the sunflowers of Provence
in primary brilliance against the bluest sky.

The landscape shifts into moiré patterns
of grapevines, their low-strung tendrils
wrapping themselves lavishly across wires,

hectare upon hectare of flowering almonds,
blossom soft and bridal, haven for bees,
segue into orange groves, all dark leaves,

citrus trees glowing with fruit,
windfall orbiting trunks like gifts,
row upon row of plants flicking by.

Geometric art, it's intensely satisfying
in an industrial kind of way, but
it speaks the language of displacement,

crop spraying, cotton seeds coated
with pesticide, the vast irrigation
schemes needed to turn the dry green.

I can feel the road pulling me onward
towards a dirt track somewhere wilder,
uncharted, to a place that defines itself.

## Cape Naturaliste

It's just you, me
and the black cockatoos
on this crumbling clifftop.
Behind us the lighthouse
solid against the early morning sky.
We walk through the last of the wildflowers,
stop to admire the convergence of elements.
Dolphins break the surface, sleek and sure,
a humpback and calf follow
ancient rhythms of migration
true as air. Our feet,
are firm on the dusty path,
grounded.

## Flotsam

Reading a borrowed novel
on the banks of the Swan River,
I take pleasure
in the beginning of a friendship,
and in the self-righteousness
of reading Henry James.
I've swum with river dolphins,
their sleek bodies just out of reach
and now I sit on a jetty,
the holiday sun warming my skin.
Suddenly the Freo Doctor
comes out of nowhere,
snatches a fistful of pages
and flings them carelessly
across the river,
waterlogged words
drift on the outgoing tide.
Such betrayals occur all the time,
but now the spine
of the relationship
is broken, unrepairable.
Meaning ebbs away
as I sit helpless on the bank
not knowing
how it all will end.

## Murasaki Shikibu in Service at the Imperial Palace, 1010

She kneels
in the midnight shadows
of her six mat room,
the stillness of the hours
seeping into her heart.
No visitor tonight,
only the sound of the wind
and the scent of a candle
long extinguished.

Her brush is wet with ink.
She holds it above a scroll,
a present from Empress Akiko.
Damp hair,
agalwood-scented,
cascades down
her silk-lined back,
and trails across the tatami floor.

She longs to dip into
the dark river of words
that once flowed within her,
but she's weary of Genji,
weary of this life.

Rising, she slides
open the shoji screen
and feels herself becoming
a silver shadow cast by the moon.

## The Scattering of Blossom

I.   *Australia*

The cherry trees are blooming
at the old POW camp in Cowra
under the guard tower,
which is just a relic now,
petals replacing barbed wire
among the ruined foundations.

In Japan it's the season
of autumn leaves,
*kouyou* followed by *rakuyou*.

Here spring rain has left
the grass lush for lambs
and the horizon
glows yellow with canola.

II.

A mass flowering of blossom
along Sakura Avenue lights the way
between camp and cemetery.

Over two hundred Japanese dead
in the Breakout, now they rest
in regimented rows
beneath a foreign soil,
death by rope, by bullet, by knife.
Hundreds went over the wire
inspired by *bushido* with its
ideals of honour from another age.

III.

in the Japanese garden
people come and go

far away in the square
the peace bell tolls


IV.     *Japan*

Lying on the manicured grass
of Rikugien Gardens,
that great Edo creation,
I gaze up into a cloud
of blossom, pale pink,
soothing, restorative,
and watch bees working
their way between flowers.

My job done, my tour group
safely back at Narita Airport,
I place my hands
on my pregnant belly
and feel the future pressing
down on me.


V.

*jindai-zakura*
supported by bamboo poles,
still blooming gloriously
after two thousand years

VI.

nightfall
we bend low to pass through
the old farmhouse gates …
he lifts his lamp
to show me cherry blossom
ethereal in the darkness


VIII.   *The Himalayas*

High in the foothills
wild cherry trees grow
into the fissures of boulders.
They make their own soil,
become one with the rock
and once a year the hillsides
become luminous with bloom
after bloom after bloom.




Footnotes

*kouyou* – leaves changing colour
*rakuyou* – fallen leaves
*bushido* – the code of honour and morals
            developed by the Japanese samurai
*jindai-zakura* – Japan's oldest cherry blossom
            tree grows in Hokuto City, Yamanashi Prefecture

## A Brief History of Umami

In the fourth century BC,
Democratus added *bitter*
to the three known tastes
of *sweet, sour* and *salty*.
No experiments needed,
he was a philosopher after all.

And so it remained
for thousands of years –
four tastes only.
But during this time,
breast milk was pretty popular
(to begin with) and the Romans
couldn't get enough garum.

In the nineteenth century
Escoffier presented his legendary
veal stock to the world,
condensing glutamate,
making it utterly delicious.

In the 1900s, Kikunae Ikeda,
a Japanese chemist,
investigating the magic of
dashi stock made from seaweed,
discovered glutamic acid.
He called it *umami*, delicious taste,
but no one in the west believed him.

Who could do without
mushrooms, sweetcorn
and cherry tomatoes,
soy sauce, parmesan and bacon?

One hundred years later,
scientists isolated a
special receptor on the tongue
for L-Glutamate and proved,
once and for all,
that there is officially
an entirely *new*
fifth taste     *umami.*

## La Cocotte Ronde

arrived today with the post,
round, enamelled, deep red,
functional, beautiful.
Who would have thought
anyone could be in raptures
over a pot? I salivate over
the thought of oven baked bread
and stovetop stews bubbling
in rich red wine.

## Walking Shadow
*After Olive Cotton's The Photographer's Shadow (1935)*

Mine is the space between light and shade.
Behind the camera my body lacks substance,
it has the texture of cirrus clouds, of wind
blown swells rolling in from Chile and Peru.
I move unnoticed over the hot sand,
always alert to the image, shifting between
shadows as vibrant as light,
shaping, framing, reframing.
There is power in the click of the shutter,
in choosing the focus, the moment.
Prospero-like, cocooned in the darkroom,
I am consumed by the alchemy of my art,
projecting my shadow over what I find,
slowly becoming my own subject.

## Florence Fisher, 1872

*After a photograph by Julia Cameron.*
*Julia Margaret Cameron: from the Victoria and Albert Museum*
*London Exhibition at the Art Gallery of NSW, 2015*

                You meet us face on.
                There is nothing
                demure about you
                though you have all
                the trappings
                of a Victorian child –
                background foliage,
                a handful of roses,
                the white dress.
                Your rosebud mouth
                may be perfect,
                but your chin
                is petulant,
                your fringe uneven,
                freckles dot your sepia face.
                Your dark defiant eyes,
                your modern gaze
                can still draw strangers
                right across the room.

## The Skating Minister

*After a painting of the Reverend Robert Walker skating* on
*Duddingston Loch, 1795, attributed to Sir Henry Raeburn*

Sombre, black-suited,
enlightened cleric,
he cuts a fine figure
across the ice.
Arms crossed,
his stockinged calves
are finely shaped.
Surging forth with grace,
is his mind fixed
on his next sermon?
On the beatitudes
or the psalms?
Or is he consumed
by the glide
of his ribboned blades
as they sweep over the freeze,
ice tingling in his lungs?
Stroking forward,
he surely succumbs to speed,
as the far shore of the loch
rises up to greet him.

## Darwin's Gardener, 1881

He moons about the garden,
does Mr Darwin,
stands before an orchid
for ten minutes or more,
stooping over his cane,
his long white beard
hardly disguising the sickness
that plagues him. I dug manure
into a bed of roses this morning,
the sweat fairly pouring off me,
and still he didn't move.

Once, Mr Darwin
asked me for a dozen worms.
The parlour maid told me
he laid them upon the piano
while the mistress played.
Something to do
with vibrations, she said.

I miss the sound of his steps
purposeful-like on the sand path
as he took Polly for a walk
every day at noon, thinking,
thinking, always thinking.
But now I believe his thoughts
have lost their way
like cabbage whites,
flittering this way and that,
settling on nothing.

But what would I know?
I have no time for mooning –
just an estate full of hedges to clip.

## Parakeets over a London Graveyard
*After the photograph Feral Spirits by Sam Hobson*

horseshoe clouds close in
over the solid
formation of headstones
adding night
to the stone cold
immobility of the past

a flock
of rose-ringed parakeets
wings over
the faint glow of streetlights
luminous, warm-blooded
consumed by motion

red-beaked immigrants
their brilliance defies
the cool earth
olive green and yellow-feathered
thousands seek roosting trees
to saturate with sound

a cherub huddles
at the base of a stone
ground-dweller, oblivious
to a parakeet sky
the birds' ghostly trails forging
a new and vibrant history

## After midnight the streets belong to the foxes
*After a photograph by Sam Hobson*

The fox stretches up
on his hind legs,
snout resting on concrete,
forefeet gripping a wall
in a suburban street.
Curious *vulpes vulpes*,
emerging from the darkness.
A burst of streetlight
illuminates his gaze,
direct, unafraid.

Forager of lanes and alleyways,
with wild orange eyes,
a hunter, the hunted.
Creature of shadow and stealth,
bin-tipping, chicken-stealing fox,
cunning beast of Aesop,
the trickster Reynard,
his russet coat shining,
hunger in his bones.

## Endangered
*Korea, 1898*

You're not even looking at the camera,
you gaze somewhere off to the left,
your moustachioed mouth downturned
with an expression of mild boredom.

You stand erect, left hand in pocket,
right hand tight around your Mauser.
The tallest by at least a foot, you are flanked
by two Korean guides. Clusters of villagers
keep a respectful distance; one boy fidgets,
his head a blur, and no one smiles.

At your feet a Siberian tiger,
two bold stripes across her belly,
the bulk of her longer than
the three of you standing side by side.
She appears to be sleeping, with
one massive paw turned upwards
and slightly open mouth,
showing a hint of incisors
that were no match for your bullets.

## Four Minutes
*Science Museum, London*

The queue twists back on itself
like a cat's cradle. Attendants check
tickets as we shuffle up the gangplank
to the display rooms full of salvaged things:
dinner plates, watches and wallets,
jewellery, silverware, deckchairs
from first class.

On the walls the disaster
is announced in bold print,
story after story –
but there are other stories
in the creases of photos,
the rip in a lifejacket,
tales deep within a lifeboat's timbers.

Two rooms back from the gift shop
is the replica of the bridge.
There under electric stars
a simulated iceberg glows
(touching is allowed)
and now the chill creeps up
your arm, numbing your senses.

At last the idea of freezing to death,
your sodden skirts dragging you down,
in frigid waters, your breath
condensing in the night air,
and the realisation that in water this cold
you have only minutes to live.

## The Sphinx Memorial, Bobbin Head

*Carved between 1926 and 1927 from sandstone as a memorial to those lives lost in the First World War by returned soldier Pte. W. T. Shirley of the 13th Battalion.*

> I like the quiet here,
> the sound of parrots
> and whipbirds,
> the flutter of fantails,
> the green and blue of bush and sky.
>
> Every day I leave the hospital,
> whistle my way down Bobbin Head Road.
> Out here everything seems brighter,
>                 more alive.
>
> The swing of the pick reassures me
> as I bring it down on rock,
> work up a sweat, catch
> my struggling breath in the shade.
> It's taking shape now,
> the Sphinx's head,
>                 feet, body
> emerging from sandstone.
>
> Egypt a far-flung memory
> of training with my mates
> across the sands of antiquity,
> the Great Sphinx of Giza
> rising out the desert
> its knowing eyes
> staring into the distance.

I can never rid myself
of the roar of the guns, always
that dull ache and the sharpness
in my lungs.
                    Lucky to make it home
I suppose, so few came back
from the Western Front –
no man without his scars.

Everyone is intent on forgetting
these days.

But some day
they will come here
           and remember.

## Endless Night
*Budapest, 1944*

His right hand cramps, fingertips
stained with ink, the strain
stiffening his neck, his shoulders.

Three clock chimes and all meaning
ebbs away. Day and night no longer
exist. Consumed by the task, he sits

in the lamp's cold glow. He needs three
hands, a hundred, to sign these visas.
He should become a *Hecatoncheire*.

But he is not the monster, just a man
armed with a pen and endless documents,
slowly waning into a world of shadow.

Resting his head on the desk, he knows
that every pause means a life lost, someone
he cannot save. Always, there is someone

he cannot save. Are there others like him
at other embassies, validating papers
at leather desks, sleepless, sore, trying

to stem the inevitable? There is not enough
time. This is the only certainty. All he can do
is take up his pen and sign and sign his name.

## Hyde Park, Sydney, 1949

To survive,
to be the only one remaining
is to sit on a park bench
in the antipodes
(no one could get farther away),
unwrap a dry paste sandwich
sealed in brown paper,
and eat but not taste.

To work in the clatter
of an airless typing pool,
the metallic racket
an antidote to thought.
*I am fine, perfectly fine.*
*Thank you for asking.*

To absorb the unforgiving heat
surrounded by the unholy
screech of cockatoos.
The weight of it all.
The impossibility of memory.
This feeling that I am
merely an assortment
of shards, badly assembled,
about to implode.

Yet, there is something substantial
about this place, its sandstone
buildings, buses and trams
careering down to the harbour.
Sunlight, spilling generously
through the figs does its best
to mask the darkness.

The wag of a Jack Russell's tail
as it noses through the undergrowth
hints at the possibility of happiness.
A neighbour heading home
whistling a familiar tune is surely
a sign that the world still turns.

And then there is the breathing,
the promise of cool autumn air,
breath after breath after breath.

## O Quam Mirabilis Est
*Hereford Cathedral*

Through the darkness they come,
along the gravel path and past
the cloisters, umbrellas drip-
ping onto ancient flagstones.

Removing their raincoats,
they settle in the choir stalls
close to the bones
of murdered Ethelbert
and Saint Thomas Cantilupe.

They quietly inhale
the scent of wax, wood and dust
as generations before them
have done. The vaulted ceilings
remain shadowed and constant.

Here, everything intensifies,
the soft patter of rain,
the echo of footfalls,
the scratch of history's quills,

the transformation of breath
into the energy of sound,
one expansive voice rising up,
visionary and numinous.


*O Quam Mirabilis Est*
Antiphon for the Creator composed by
Hildegard of Bingen (1098 – 1179)

# Le Stryge
Notre-Dame de Paris, April 2020

*The devil, the proud spirit, cannot endure to be mocked*
*Sir Thomas More*

   *Mon dieu*, I am dying of ennui.
   For nearly two hundred years
   I have leant my elbows onto
   the cold stone of the north tower,
   poked my tongue out at the world.
   Neither medieval, nor a gargoyle
   with a purpose, I'm an impotent
   vampire, chimera, horned child-
   poisoner, monkey-faced creation
   of Viollet-le-Duc, doomed
   to survey the streets of Paris
   in the cold, the rain, the blazing sun.

   I long for the bustle of the Second Empire
   and La Belle Époque's cars and carriages.
   Later, bombs blazed in exhilarating explosions,
   German tanks grinding their way into the city,
   years of jackboot oppression, then liberation,
   revolution and riot. This city is a place
   where things happen. Even in peacetime
   a blazing fire ravaged this very roof.

   Now there is nothing, *rien*, the city deserted.
   La Seine, sluggish and impervious,
   flows past empty streets and empty squares
   in a living nightmare. I, Le Stryge,
   have become an object of derision,
   some idiot gilding me with a surgical mask.
   Even in my heart of stone, I have feelings.

Would anyone notice if I stretched
my sculpted wings like the dirty clouds
of *pigeons de ville* and shook off this malaise,
launching myself into the breeze high above
the city, finally making my escape?

## Basement Blues

Intent on his twilight errand
to the grocery store, the boy
collides with an unruly cloud
of jazz notes. The beat tugs him
down the street, his shoes pound
the rhythm on the pavement until
he is sprinting past brothels
and streetwalkers, stopping only
when he reaches the source.

He stands in the blue shadows,
trumpet notes bursting in his brain,
the sax a sparkler in staccato conversation,
the roar of brass reverberating
around city streets with only
the double bass to ground it,
pulsing into the hazy night.

The window shines yellow in the darkness,
keyhole into a world of sound.
He smells the jazz, the bodies,
the drink. He sees himself inside,
lips pressed against the trumpet,
lost in the rhythm, never turning back.

## Old Violin

I.
Shaped from the spruce forests
of Bohemia before the First World War,
you are from the age of the craftsman,
handmade in a dimly lit workshop
by a luthier working for a pittance.
He placed you in a sack,
a jangling package of possibilities,
strapped it to his body,
and trudged along the steep and
well-worn path into Germany.
I imagine it was winter
and he wore snowshoes
to save him from sinking deep
into the drifts.

II.
Whose student fingers
worked their way across your fingerboard?
Whose child did you belong to?
Were they diligent in their practice
or were you easily cast aside?
You survived upheaval, war, madness,
so many musicians sent to the camps.
I like to think of you during the bombing,
tucked away in your case
in someone's cellar,
the tautness released from your bow,
cold and a little damp, but safe.

III.
Decades later, in a musty workshop
£200 exchanged hands
and you were mine.
A full size violin at twelve years old,
a rite of passage.
You survived the rough treatment
of my petulant teens,
the poor fingering, attempts at vibrato,
the frustration, the resentment,
always did what you were told,
lay mute for years and years.

IV.
Now, half a world away,
restored and restrung,
your timbre is resonant,
mellow, knowing
as you sing
        and you sing
                and you sing.

## Caught

When I hear
that my friend is dying,
I leave, driving the Toyota
along the road north to the coast
past shops, the rubbish tip,
the Bahai temple
to vistas of grey-green bush
and a hazy horizon.

The unbarred sky
allows each wave set
to roll in,
wind-driven, foam-crested.
The terracotta sand
radiates heat
to burn the soles.

The sea is unseasonably warm
for April and I wade in
without hesitation.
Yet today I lack
the courage to swim out
beyond the breakers,
allowing myself to be tossed
here and there in the shore break
by surging waves
ricocheting from the sandbank,
churning sand, tangled seaweed,
in the no space
between the elements.
Caught.

## Aftermath

flying home
he stows her ashes
in the check-in luggage

writing the eulogy
all day long bees forage
in the lavender

things said
and not said …
memorial service

country churchyard
the insistent caw
of a raven

the wake over
he accelerates onto
the open road

**Night Vision**

We cannot see
the colour of the stars
with the naked eye,
moonlight mutes
our view of the world.
Living behind drawn blinds
we are oblivious
to the expansiveness of the sky.

Everyday vision
refracts light,
mirrors the outlines
of those closest to us.
Familiarity
renders us colour blind
even when we live, lie
beside our lovers
for more than half our lives.

## Myopia

Without glasses
you enter the world of the half-
known, where every familiar shape
becomes the sum of itself.

After years of corrected vision,
to take down one's guard
is to lose all hard edges.

Skirting boards bleed into walls,
a dark shape scurries across the floorboards
only the way a cockroach can
and the fan throws out its arms
spinning shadows across the room.

## Orbit

Sometimes the world slips
out of kilter. Only a fraction,
but enough
to keep you awake at night,
your mind spiralling through
infinite anxieties,
the journal beside your bed
indecipherable.
Spinning in an irregular orbit,
at odds with circadian rhythms,
you are not quite yourself.
The constant friction
drags you down.
All you need
is to walk out one morning,
mist rising from the valley,
and something will come
at you, head on,
crashing through the canopy.

A Powerful Owl,
all barred feathers and hooked beak,
will land in the heart of a blue gum,
its talons curved meaningfully
over a limb. It will regard
you with deep amber eyes
and muscular wings will test the air.
Launching into flight,
it will head straight for you,
the sheer weight of its body
knocking you right back
where you need to be.

## Scenic

The pay binoculars
look out to sea in all weathers,
swivel head waiting
to swallow cold metal,
waiting to feel the warmth
of a human face pressed close.

Fixed, they focus us,
narrow our perspective
to stop and really see,
not just a mass of water,
green-hued or bottomless blue,

but a single wave, foamy crest
curling into itself, the shadow
of submerged rocks, a surfer,
a swimmer, a whale, a boat,
the swirls of low sweeping clouds.

## In Praise of Ocean Swimmers

In praise

of the early risers,
the swimming cap-donners,
the cold water bravers,
religiously tackling the swells,
duck diving under each set,
through foam and wash and weed
striving to *get out the back,*

of those who swim
round the headland
elegantly stroking their way
across the bay with their
sweeping arms and flutter kicks
powering through the waves
over unseen fins,

of those who glide
back in with the surf
rise, cap in hand,
water dripping,
smiling beatific smiles
as the sun kicks it way
up from the horizon.

## The Gift

An unexpected day off,
phone battery flat,
sunshine, a chair in the shade,
the call of an unknown bird,
a chainsaw far enough away
to sound like music.

## A Brief Catalogue of Joy

turning off the news
the world opens up
to birdsong


bush track
my collie springs
into the creek


cascades …
a water dragon clambers
into sunlight


a vase of windflowers
on the kitchen table
letter from a friend


home delivery
a box of books
with my name on them


full moon
my daughter reads me
a story

## Publication Credits

'Emergence' Second Prize in ANU Health Poetry Prize Competition 2017. *Meniscus*, October vol. 5 no. 2 2017

'Natural History Museum' Commended, Society of Women Writers NSW Poetry Competition 2003

'Ashridge Forest' *Not Very Quiet*, no. 7 2020

'On Wonder' *Australian Poetry Journal*, no. 7.2 2017

'A dragonfly' *Quadrant*, vol. 57 no. 1/2 2013, *The School Magazine, Touchdown* April 2016, Issue No. 3

'Expansions' *Australian Poetry Anthology* 2016

'Citizen Science' *Meanjin*, vol. 79 no. 2 2020

'Overflow' *Meanjin*, vol. 82 no. 2 2023

'Bathroom Orchid' *Australian Poetry Journal*, vol. 5 no. 2 2015

'All in the Timing' *Meanjin*, vol 78 no. 3 2019

'Crossing the Harbour Bridge' Commended Yeats Poetry Prize of Australia 2014, *Australian Poetry Anthology* 2015

'Whale Psalm' *Joy: Poems from the 2017 ACU Prize for Poetry*

'Fitzroy Falls' *Catchment – Poetry of Place*, no. 2 2024

'A Walk in the Fog and Snow, Kinglake, After a Photograph by Lloyd Godman' *Catchment –Poetry of Place*, no. 2 2024

'Fingal Spit' *Stylus Lit*, no.16 2024

'Westward' *Not Very Quiet*, no. 5 2019

'Murasaki Shikibu in Service at the Imperial Palace', 1010 *Southerly*, vol. 65 no. 2 2005

'A Brief History of Umami' *Quadrant*, vol. 59 no. 6 2015

'Walking Shadow' *Meniscus*, vol. 12 no. 1 2024

'Darwin's Gardener, 1881' Winner of the Society of Women Writers NSW Poetry Competition 2008, *Images* 2011 – 2012

'Parakeets Over a London Graveyard' *Meanjin*, vol. 76 no. 3 2017

'Endangered, Korea 1898' *Southerly*, vol. 65 no. 2 2025

'Four Minutes' *Poetrix*, no. 27 2006

'Endless Night' *Generosity: Poems from the 2020 ACU Prize for Poetry*

'Hyde Park, Sydney, 1949' *Solace: Poems from the 2019 ACU Prize for Poetry*

'Le Stryge' *Not Very Quiet*, no. 8 2021

'Orbit' Second Place, Tom Collins Poetry Prize 2017

'The Gift' *The Canberra Times* Saturday 4th February, 2023

'A Brief Catalogue of Joy' *The Haiku Hecameron*, Girasole Press (2020) ed. Scott Mason

Vanessa Proctor

Image credit | Natalie Barclay

www.ingramcontent.com/pod-product-compliance
Lightning Source LLC
Chambersburg PA
CBHW061751070526
44585CB00025B/2856